Reflections of His Heart

~A Heart Like Mine~

Written by
Cypress Ministries

Reflections of His Heart

Published by Faith Books Publishing
ISBN 978-0-9834135-4-7

Reflections of
His Heart

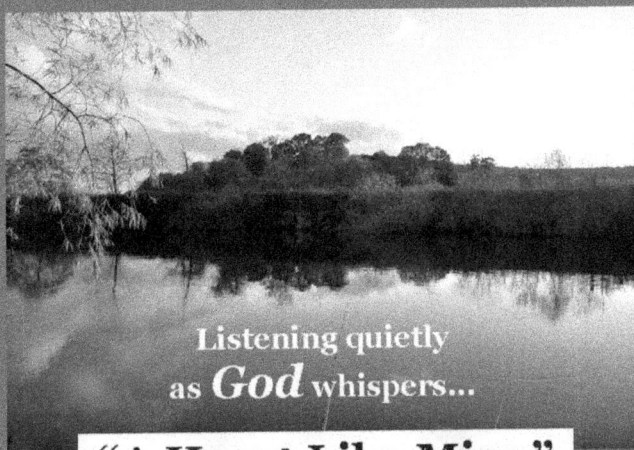

Listening quietly
as *God* whispers...

"A Heart Like Mine"

Series Written by
Cypress Ministries

DEDICATION

This writing is dedicated to our heavenly Father
who so often reminds me to
"Be still and know that *IN ALL THINGS* I AM GOD"

To His Son, who is truly the Author and Finisher of my
faith, and it is in Him that I am able
to find strength each day,

To His Holy Spirit who teaches me, leads me,
and tugs at my heart when I don't know where to go.

When I stumble with "Who am I?"
the Lord picks me back up with
**"Who has given man his mouth,
and makes him deaf or mute?
Who gives him sight or makes him blind?
Is it not I, the LORD?
Now go; I will help you speak
and will teach you what to say."**
(Scripture reference: Exod. 4:11-12)

It is in Christ's name that I give all glory to God, who is the
true Author of these words that I have penned.
I give thanks to Him for I am simply a vessel and humbled
that each morning when I rise He gives me a heart for His
Word to write down. And so with a trembling heart,
I simply say, "Thank You, God."

Table of Contents

As you see God's wisdom and understanding, listen quietly as he whispers
to you from His heart concerning His
will, plans, and purposes for your life.

I will sprinkle clean water on you, and you shall be clean from all your uncleannesses, and from all your idols I will cleanse you. And I will give you a new heart, and a new spirit I will put within you. And I will remove the heart of stone from your flesh and give you a heart of flesh. And I will put my Spirit within you, and cause you to walk in my statutes and be careful to obey my rules.

Ezek. 36:25–27 (ESV)

INTRODUCTION

THE LORD God calls us and draws us to Him. He seeks to form a close personal relationship with each of us. He sent His Son to bridge the gap between Him and us. And then He sent His Holy Spirit to live inside of us, so that we may be one with Him, and to know His Heart.

However, when He, the Spirit of truth, has come, He will guide you into all truth; for He will not speak on His own *authority,* but whatever He hears He will speak; and He will tell you things to come. He will glorify Me, for He will take of what is Mine and declare *it* to you. All things that the Father has are Mine. Therefore I said that He will take of Mine and declare *it* to you (John 16:13-15 NKJV).

Listen with your heart as our heavenly Father calls you by name *(HIS)*, and speaks to you as if saying, *"If you will let me, I will cleanse you and create in you a new heart. If you will let me, I will heal you, restore you, and comfort you. If you will let me, I will give you a new way of thinking and create in you a heart like mine.... Come lay your burdens down and learn to walk with me, and you will find that all you need, I AM."*

Introduction is taken from

A Worshiper's Heart written by Cypress Ministries.

And I will give them one heart,
and a new spirit I will put
within them.
I will remove the heart of stone
from their flesh and give them
a heart of flesh, that they may walk
in My statutes and keep
My ordinances and do them.
Then they will be My people,
and I shall be their God.

Ezek. 11:19–20 (ESV)

Chapter 1

THE LORD

When Paul and Barnabus were teaching at Antioch in Pisidia, Paul started with a recap of history. He reminded the people there of how, toward the end of Samuel's life, the people of long ago wanted a king, so Saul was crowned. But when King Saul refused to listen and obey God, he lost his kingdom. Paul quoted what the Lord had said to Samuel in reference to David, **"And when he had removed him, he raised up David to be their king, of whom he testified and said, 'I have found in David the son of Jesse a man after my heart, who will do all my will'"** (Acts 13:22 ESV).

Was David perfect? NO. Did David make mistakes? YES! But what pleased God about him was David's willingness to be a vessel for God. David was a man. By this I mean simply that he was HUMAN. David made mistakes and at times sinned. But he truly always had a heart for God. When he was in despair he sought the Lord. When he needed guidance he sought the Lord.

And when he messed up—when he sinned—he sought the Lord. David had a surrendered heart to the Lord. David opened his heart and allowed God to work in him and through him, thus creating in David a heart like **His**, with David becoming known as a man whose mistakes were forgiven and being called by God Himself, *"A man after my heart."*

What I find totally inspiring is that when Samuel told King Saul that God had "sought out a man of his own heart" (read 1 Samuel 13:14), this was BEFORE David had been anointed by Samuel, and BEFORE David had even had a chance to grow up! Remember that when Samuel did go to find this "man," David was still a young boy. David truly was the CHOSEN one, not Saul. The people wanted a king-- what they didn't realize was that God had one for them-- but they didn't want to wait. The problem was David needed time to grow up, and the people wound getting second best in the mean time, because they wanted someone "now."

When God told Samuel to anoint the boy child, God called him "A man after my own heart." The Lord had already viewed all the days of David's life. He knew the times David would falter, and He knew the times David would fall to sin, but God also knew what would truly be in David's heart all of his life. God knew that in the depths of David's heart was and would always be a heart for God.

God knew He could entrust the leadership responsibility of His people to David. My quick question to you is, what is God entrusting you with?

This thought about David reminds me of another time the Lord spoke to someone already "knowing." Look, if you will, at Luke 22:31–34, Jesus told Peter that Satan had requested to "sift" Peter, and that God had allowed it.

Jesus told Peter that he would falter, but Jesus also told Peter that he (Peter) would stand back up: *"When you return to me..."* In essence

Jesus was telling Peter, *"Satan is going to sift you like flour, you are going to scrape your knees falling down, but I already know you are going to stand back up, and you will be stronger for it. And when you return to Me, help your brothers."*

You might wonder why God would allow this—because as strong as Peter was, he was also arrogant. The Lord needed the arrogance to be shaken out of Peter so that Peter would no longer be full of himself but full of God.

Remember, Peter was a born leader—he was a successful businessman (or fisherman). Peter had natural strength. God needed to realign Peter inside, so He allowed Satan to put Peter through the ringer.

But you have to also know that if God hadn't been certain that ultimately Peter's faith would win and that Peter would come back stronger than before as a humble man, God would never have allowed it. God will not let us be tested past our breaking point. If God is allowing something, then you have to know that good will come from it. And if it feels as if you are breaking in half, then hold tighter to the hand of God, because *HE IS THERE WITH YOU EVERY STEP OF THE WAY*. Don't *YOU* turn away from Him.

Jesus knew that day (referred to in Luke 22) that Peter would say three times that night that he (Peter) didn't know Him. But Jesus also knew that this same Peter would set his world on fire, lead people to Him, and go to the grave witnessing for Him.

Jesus knew what Peter's true heart was BEFORE Peter ever knew what would happen. It was the same way with David. It is why long before David would be king, God could already say, "This man is a man after my own heart." God called David a man while he was still just a boy. And God spoke in 1 Samuel 13:14 as if David was *already* appointed—not would be—but as "Is." Meaning it was already a done deal. It is the same way God spoke of Isaac to Abraham, as if Isaac already was. (Read Romans 4:17) Calling Abraham a father of MANY before he physically was a father of one. (*God even called Abraham His friend* (see Isaiah 41:8). God already knew. God stated what He had planned. And God did what He said He would do.

He did so with Abraham. He did so with David. And He did so again with Peter. God looked into these men, past these men, and saw what they would become and who they were *in Him*, and knew they would keep hearts *for Him*.

Is that what **you** long for? Is that what your heart is aching for? Then, beloved friend, know that God is drawing you and working in you. Believe that God is trying to reach down into the crevices to cleanse you. Take a deep breath and slowly exhale; be still and just listen.

Could it be-- is it possible-- that at this very moment God is whispering in you,

> *"Let me create in YOU*
> *a heart like Mine."*

Chapter 2

T H E One of the greatest joys in letting God renew our hearts is the peace we have when faced with sudden difficulties. Read with me Psalm 112:7: "**He is not afraid of bad news; his heart is firm, trusting in the LORD**" (ESV).

L O R D When God is the lord of our hearts, we won't fall into sudden fear when something unexpected is thrown into our laps. We can hold steadfast that God is with us in these situations and will see us past them.

So how do we let God create in us a heart like His? By spending daily time in quietness with Him and His Word. We have to allow God to come in and root out in our hearts all that isn't of Him, so that He can prepare our hearts and then sow in us what *IS* His.

Just as a farmer will plow up the ground before planting seeds, God will do the same thing in our hearts. "**But you, O mountains of Israel,**

shall shoot forth your branches and yield your fruit to my people Israel, for they will soon come home. For behold, I am for you, and I will turn to you, and you shall be tilled and sown" (Ezek. 36:8–9 ESV).

I also like how the New Century Version Bible states Ezekiel 36:8–9:

> **"But you, mountains of Israel, will grow branches and fruit for my people, who will soon come home. I am concerned about you; I am on your side. You will be plowed, and seed will be planted in you."**

Friend, know that you and I are "Israel." When we accept Christ as our Lord and Savior, we become a member of God's family, part of *HIS CHOSEN PEOPLE*. For all practical purposes we can view ourselves as "the children of Jacob, the family of Israel." The "mountains" of the land are our hearts. And from our hearts, we are meant to bear fruit, much fruit, the kind of fruit that will last our lifetime and pass into our families and generations after us.

Keep in mind, we can never fool God. He knows when our desires for Him are real. Turn to Hosea 7:13–15:

"Woe to them, for they have strayed from me! Destruction to them, for they have rebelled against me! I would redeem them, but they speak lies against me. They do not cry to me from the heart, but they wail upon their beds; for grain and wine they gash themselves; they rebel against me. Although I trained and strengthened their arms, yet they devise evil against me" (ESV).

Another verse that comes to mind is from Psalm 78:35–37:

"They would remember that God was their Rock. That God Most High had saved them. But their words were

**false, and their tongues lied to him.
Their hearts were not really loyal to
God; they did not keep his agree-
ment"** (NCV).

God draws us to Him, and when we are truly
sincere in our desires for Him, He will prepare
our hearts to receive His gift of grace and salva-
tion through His Son.

God will plow us and remove the stubborn
stones of selfish thinking and root up anything
else that has started growing and doesn't belong.
Then Christ heals us, and the Holy Spirit comes to
live inside of us, sealing us with redemption. This
is the very foundation of belief:

That God *is God.* That Christ came
down and died on the cross for us, forever
bridging the gap between us and God, so
that through Christ we may be *healed
and forgiven.* And that His Holy Spirit
is real and lives inside of us, so that we
truly become a child of God. Christ looked

over the span of time into the pits of hell and declared to the enemy about me (and *about YOU*), *"This one IS MINE. This person belongs to me."*

I love what God says in Ezekiel 34:31–13:

"Then they will know that I, the LORD their God, am with them. The nation of Israel will know that they are my people, says the Lord GOD. You, my human sheep, are the sheep I care for, and I am your God, says the Lord GOD" (NCV).

And in the process of all of this, our hearts are renewed. We begin to see others as He sees them. We are able to love others more because God loves them. We are able to be more and give more to others emotionally and spiritually because God's love flows through us to others. We begin to have more understanding of what God wants to do through our lives. And we can start to see God's purposes and plans for us in reaching others for Him. When our hearts are lined up with His, we start seeing more spiritual fruit growing in our lives because **He** is growing in us. His Holy Spirit begins to flow through us, and we can see more through the eyes of Christ in our surroundings.

We have three boys, and when one of them comes in mad and upset about something one of the others has done it sometimes is hard to get a word in edgewise until the upset child has calmed down enough to listen. It reminds me of Elijah in 1 Kings 19.

When God asked Elijah why he was there (in other words: why had Elijah come out into the desert and ended up on the mountain in distress), somehow I don't think Elijah just calmly stated, "Oh, you know..." I think that when God asked Elijah why he was there, Elijah took all the grief, frustration, and fear bottled up inside and said, **"HERE'S WHY..."** Hence the three storms in the valley God had Elijah witness before speaking to him again.

For me, I think the three storms often represent all the turmoil that comes into our lives and into our circumstances until we get to a point where, like Elijah, we just can't handle anymore.

Or like with one of the boys, I will ask them, "What happened?" and then I have to wait for them to vent it all out before I can really talk to them in a way that they can, *and will*, listen to. I think that is often how we are with God. We have so many things happening, and we keep it inside thinking, "If I can just hold it together until..." Sometimes God has to let us get past ourselves before we can just lie down and be at a place where we can truly listen to Him.

If you look at 1 Kings 19:9–18, first God asks, and Elijah replies. Then the three storms happen, but afterward, in calmness, God asks again, *"Elijah, why are you here?"* I think when God asked the second time, Elijah was "spent" and at a place inside where he was calmer and could not just hear God but could really listen to what God wanted to say to him. And do you know what God told him? In a sense, God told Elijah, *"Hey, your*

21

job is not over. I still have people that need me, that have been loyal to me, and I am sending you to them to help them for me."

My friend, God told Elijah exactly how many people were in the area where Elijah was being sent who needed and were waiting for God's help. Do you know what that means? It means that in the center of a place that seemed to be completely against God, the Lord knew exactly how many people still had a heart for Him, where they were, and how to get to them! The same is as true now as it was back then. God knows who His people are, ones who truly have a heart for Him, even if that heart is buried in mud and filth. He knows how to get to them, restore them, and heal them. My friend, God knows how to get to *you* too, and if need be, He knows how to send someone to YOU to help and reach YOU.

But you know what else?
God knows how to work in YOU so that
He can use you to reach someone else.

You do not have to be a pastor, preacher, worship leader, or even in ministry to be a vessel for God to use to reach someone lost and hurting. All you have to have is a heart – a *heart willing to be made like His*. My friend, know that God will do the real work. He just looks for someone that is willing to say, "Here, take mine. Use me." God's Word says in Zechariah 4.6: **"Not by might, nor by power, but by my Spirit, says the Lord of hosts"** (ESV).

Would you be willing? Are you willing to let God come in and work in you so He can work through you? Are you willing to let Him take your heart and make it like His?

It doesn't matter what kind of pit God pulls you from; all it takes is a sincere heart. *"Lord, create in me a **New Heart**, a **Clean Heart**. Lord come in and create in me a **Pure Heart"** (Ps. 51:6). *When we do this, God steps in and does the rest.*

When we seek to know God's Heart, He works in us to create in us a Heart like His that is reflected to others around us as He works to draw them closer to Him.

> *For I have given you an example,*
> *that you also should do just as*
> *I have done to you.*
> *Truly, truly, I say to you,*
> *a servant is not greater than*
> *his master, nor is a messenger*
> *greater than the one who sent him.*
> *If you know these things,*
> *blessed are you if you do them.*
>
> *John 13:15–17 (ESV)*

Chapter 3

One amazing gift from the Lord is the way His Holy Spirit will speak to us and enlighten our hearts to His Word as we read the Bible. God's Word will literally become a light to us and in us as we open up our hearts to His voice and His Holy Spirit teaching us. As we grow, we begin to see our reflection in His Word. If we sin, His Word will convict us, but His Word will also give us direction and guidance. As we come to know Him and He starts to redefine our hearts, we will begin to see our desires and our heart's longings in His Word. That is because He is speaking to us and planting His desires in us. Then His dreams for us become *OUR DREAMS for us.* As we read His Words with the help of God's Holy Spirit, His Words begin to reflect what is in our hearts. It is almost as if we are looking in a mirror. Do you know why? Because of God Himself, and the desire of *HIS HEART,* that is being reflected back to us and *in us*. It truly is like looking in a mirror.

The problem is so often we become "guilty of looking in the mirror and then going off and forgetting what we see" (James 1:23). A real test of faith is when we are willing to act in obedience to what God shows as His will for us. So it is important to stay in God's Word regularly and apply what He teaches us.

God truly delights in having a personal relationship with us and desires to speak directly to us, but it is up to us to listen. When we fill our minds, thoughts, and ears with a lot of "outside noise," it will hinder our ability to hear within our spirit when God speaks to us. When we are constantly in a whirlwind, it will dim our senses to God's Holy Spirit softly speaking to us. We have to make an effort to come aside and quietly sit before God. The busier our lives are, the more important it is to find the time, or to *make* the time, to come before God for peace and direction. It's what anchors us so that when storms rage, we also can with confidence "sleep in the front of the boat, knowing that we to will make it to the other side of the lake." (See Matthew 8 and Mark 4.)

God's Word says in Joshua 1 to mediate on His Word day and night. And in Proverbs 4, His Word says to keep what He tells us in our hearts and not to let go of it.

Turn with me to Luke 4:4: **"And Jesus answered him, 'It is written, Man shall not live by bread alone'"** (ESV). Jesus was quoting a verse in Deuteronomy 8, when Moses was talking to the Israelites just before crossing the Jordan River.

My friend, this is what we also need to remember. That we, too, do not live on bread alone. But we *NEED* God's Word every day if we are to stay connected to Him. We need to know what His Word says and to have His Word firmly planted in us so that we can stand against distractions and false leading.

If we want a solid relationship with our heavenly Father, then we have to make the time, and take the time, to let Him speak to us and lead us in His direction. And His Holy Spirit will help. I have learned that if I will spend time with God first in the mornings and take what He teaches me with me throughout the day, then I can follow in His purpose for me so much more. I have also learned that if I will make the time at some point in the evening to reconnect with Him and come back to His Word I read that morning, it stays stronger in me. His Word becomes clearer to me, and I don't forget as easily what He is showing me. I find that I have better insight and direction. And when God brings others alongside me, I have a stronger sensitivity to the Holy Spirit's prompting about how to help them or to better interact with them. When we can see others from God's heart, it helps us to view them with His understanding and not our own.

I have learned that when we let God lead us and work in our hearts to make them more like His, we can hear more clearly as He speaks to us about His will, plans, and purposes for our life— and even more importantly how He wants to work through our lives for His glory. As we open up to God, He will share His Heart with us concerning people around us. God will show us *HIS HEART* for our loved ones, our families and friends, and others that come alongside us. He will show us what He sees in them and how He wants to work through our lives to reach them and bring them into His fold. Just a few verses to look at in your quiet time regarding this would be Amos 3:7, Luke 18:15–16, John 4:27, John 11:1–44, and John 15:15–17.

The Lord invites each of us into a stronger and more personal relationship with Him. Jesus prayed in John 17 that His followers would be one with the Father *just as He was one with the Father*. But His prayer didn't stop there. He went on to pray that "*ALL Believers*" become one with Him and the Father.

"I do not ask for these only, but also for those who will believe in me through their word, that they may all be one, just as you, Father, are in me, and I in you, that they also may be in us, so that the world may believe that you have sent me. The glory that you have given me I have given to them,

that they may be one even as we are one, I in them and you in me, that they may become perfectly one, so that the world may know that you sent me and loved them even as you loved me" (John 17:20–23 ESV).

Won't you open up your heart and allow Him to work in you so that the desires and love in your heart become a reflection of His?

"Come higher, and go deeper."

Spend time seeking the Lord in His Word and listen quietly as you find out what He wants to do in YOUR life and through Your life to reach others so that *"His kingdom comes."*

♥♥♥♥♥♥♥♥♥♥♥♥

And it begins with a simple, quiet surrender to God:

"Yes Lord, make Your heart mine.
Let Your will become mine.
Yes, Father God, come
and be Lord in my life."

Chapter 4

In closing, I would like to leave you with Paul's prayer:

"That is why since I heard about your faith in the Lord Jesus and your love for all God's people, I have not stopped giving thanks to God for you. I always remember you in my prayers, asking the God of our Lord Jesus Christ, the glorious Father, to give you a spirit of wisdom and revelation so that you will know him better. I pray also that you will have greater understanding in your heart so you will know the hope to which he has called us and that you will know how rich and glorious are the blessings God has promised his holy people. And you will know that God's power is very great for us who believe. That power is the same as the great strength God used to raise Christ from the dead and put him at his right side in the heavenly world. God has put Christ over all rulers, authorities, powers, and kings, and every title that can be given, not only in this world but also the next. God put everything under his power and made him the head over everything for the church, which is Christ's body. The church is filled with Christ, and Christ fills everything in every way" (Eph. 1:15-23 NCV).

I encourage you to take the time to re-write this prayer of Paul's into your own prayer journal. Put your name into it and make it a personal prayer from you to God. Also, you can create a personal prayer from this for each of your loved ones. *There really is power in praying God's own words back to Him when we stand and claim them over ourselves and those close to us.*

PART 4: SURRENDERING A HEART

> *Search me, O God,*
> *and know my heart!*
> *Try me and know*
> *my thoughts!*
> *And see if there be any*
> *grievous way in me,*
> *and lead me*
> *in the way everlasting!*
>
> *Psalms 139:23-24 (ESV)*

Thoughts to Consider

- How often do you read the Bible?

- Does God's Word seem to speak to you?

- Do you ever experience times when what you read in His Word seems to reflect the VERY THING in your heart and what you have been thinking?

- In what ways would *you like* to see God work in you?

- In what ways are *you willing* to let God change you?

- In what area of your life do *you need* to see God's hand in?

Please keep in mind: YES there really is a difference between LIKE, WILLING and NEED.

Seven Day Challenge

Every day for one full week, spend a designated amount of time that you feel you can truly commit to in quietness before God, and let Him bring and work peace into your heart.

Go with an open heart and let Him lead you in your special time together. Surrender your heart to the Lord, with an open mind, ask that He bless your time together, ask Him to work in you and prepare your heart for what He would like to show you. Be willing to let Him come and plow up the things in your heart that are not of Him. Have courage to ask Him to show you things He may want you to let go of.

GOAL: what is the amount of time you are going to try and set aside each day for the next seven days to spend special quality time with the Lord?

Where are you going to "go and meet with the Lord as your and His "Special Place"?

Day 1) **Date:** _____

♥ How much time were you able to spend?

♥ Did you pray, read the Bible, sit in quietness, or find yourself in heartfelt worship?

♥ What areyour thoughts about this time with God?

♥ Was there a specific verse that seemed to light up in your heart?

Day 2) **Date:** _____

♥ How much time were you able to spend?

♥ Did you pray, read the Bible, sit in quietness, or find yourself in heartfelt worship?

♥ What areyour thoughts about this time with God?

♥ Was there a specific verse that seemed to light up in your heart?

Day 3) **Date:** _____

♥ How much time were you able to spend?

♥ Did you pray, read the Bible, sit in quietness, or find yourself in heartfelt worship?

♥ What areyour thoughts about this time with God?

♥ Was there a specific verse that seemed to light up in your heart?

Day 4) **Date:** _____

♥ How much time were you able to spend?

♥ Did you pray, read the Bible, sit in quietness, or find yourself in heartfelt worship?

♥ What areyour thoughts about this time with God?

♥ Was there a specific verse that seemed to light up in your heart?

Day 5) **Date:** _____

♥ How much time were you able to spend?

♥ Did you pray, read the Bible, sit in quietness, or find yourself in heartfelt worship?

♥ What areyour thoughts about this time with God?

♥ Was there a specific verse that seemed to light up in your heart?

Day 6) **Date:** _____

♥ How much time were you able to spend?

♥ Did you pray, read the Bible, sit in quietness, or find yourself in heartfelt worship?

♥ What areyour thoughts about this time with God?

♥ Was there a specific verse that seemed to light up in your heart?

Day 7) **Date:** _____

   ♥ How much time were you able to spend?

   ♥ Did you pray, read the Bible, sit in quiet-ness, or find yourself in heartfelt worship?

   ♥ What areyour thoughts about this time with God?

   ♥ Was there a specific verse that seemed to light up in your heart?

After waiting for a full week of seeking God's desire for you, come back and work on the following questions:

- What is the biggest impression you feel God working in you?

- In the total quietness of your heart, what does God seem to be saying He wants for you?

- And in total honesty, what does God want FROM you? Are there things (or even other people) He wants you to lay down?

- In totally honest reflection, what do you see is the biggest change God wants to work in you?

- Are you willing?

- Does it scare you, make you somewhat nervous, or is it exciting to you?

Personal Thoughts and Prayer Space:

Part 5: About this Series

Reflections of His Heart: A Heart Like Mine, is the introduction to our *Reflections series* which has been created to help you to spend more meaningful time with God, as you spend time IN HIS WORD. Thereby growing in a deeper relationship with Him, and learning how to reflect His heat to others.

It is also our hope that this series will help you to not only have a better understanding of His Word, but to see how it truly does connect with our lives today, and how to apply it to everyday living.

When the ground is parched and a nice summer shower comes along, everything is refreshed. The same is with our weary soles when we allow the refreshing LIVING WATERS to pour out on us.

However there also comes a time when we need to "go deeper" and FEED on His Word, in order to grow into mature Christians.

So in light of this we have set up our Reflections series as two different 12-month guides:

(1) Our "Reflections of His Heart Journaling Guides" are created to help deepen your devotional time with God, and include a daily reading plan that will take you through the whole Bible in one year, and has daily journaling pages for your morning meditations and your evening reflections. These journals are set up as monthly guides beginning in January, However, since these are geared more for your quiet devotional time, you can actually start them any month of the year (just pick up the "current month's journal"), if you don't mind starting some of the Books of the Bible in mid-stream since many of them are carried over (starting in one month, and then finishing in the next month). These can be used your own every day devotional time, or as a companion to your personal study time while going through our study guides.

(2) Is our *Reflections Study Guides*. These 24 guides (12 for the OT and 12 for the NT) are created to take you deeper into God's Word as you spend quiet time with Him. Though not a full-blown synthetic study, these do give you Biblical insights as to what is being read each day. These guides also include a daily reading guide and study pages, as you walk through the Bible with God. The reflective questions are to help you to see how the truth of God's Word can be connected to our everyday life (as we learn to live our lives from His perspective) and we grow in our relationship with Him. *(It is suggested that you start with volume 1, in order to be able to keep up with the story/study line. However if you don't mind starting in the middle of a Biblical Book, you can use the 12 volumes to match a monthly calendar.)*

Making the Most of Your Quiet Time

**The brothers immediately sent Paul
and Silas away by night to Berea,
and when they arrived they went into
the Jewish synagogue. Now these Jews
were more noble than those in
Thessalonica; they received the word
with all eagerness, examining the Scriptures daily to see if these things were so.**
(Acts 17:10-11 ESV)

There are two main ways to sit down with your Bible. And actually, it is important to have BOTH for a
healthy Spiritual diet. (I smile as I write this because you
are probably wondering, *"Huh?"*) The two ways to study,
which we are going to look at is (1) Devotionally, and (2)
Book Study/Survey for Understanding.

The first way to approach your study time is "Devotionally" and there actually two parts to this: the 1st is
when you sit and read His Word to simply let it refresh
you. This is when you are open to just receiving a fresh
new Word God might want to share with you, and 2nd,
this is a time for Him to nourish you, and prepare you

for instructions, direction, and personal application. Devotional study is more to feed our hearts, and to be able to see a reflection of God's heart, which deepens our relationship with Him.

➢ The word "Devotional comes from the word "Devotion" which means: dedication, conse-cration, worship, and sincere attachment. This type of study leads to an increase of dedi-cation and consecration to God. It also leads to a more personal relationship with God and helps us to worship Him more in our hearts and with our lives. This type of study also helps us to lean key principles that can be ap-plied to our lives, helping us to not only be hearers of the Word, but doers of the Word, as well.

  o During this time, you will want to pick: key verses, record insight into this Word that God is giving you, respond to personal application so that the les-son is brought out into your own life, and personal prayer regarding what God is teaching you through this verse. (We offer several devotionals in a different section of this book, for you to consider.)

- *Questions to consider during this time: is God giving you an example to follow? Is there an error to avoid? Is there a duty to perform, or is there a promise to claim?*

When you are devotionally reading, this is a good time to use your reading guide to follow whatever reading plan God has directed you to. This is also a good time to just absorb His Word as you read, and make note of any verses that God highlights to you, and also to write them down to meditate on them later throughout the day. Then the 2nd part of this devotional time, is where you can use this time to look up any Cross references for these verses, and prayfully ask God to work them into you, and help you to understand how they apply to your life, and how He would have you to stand on them. This is also a good time to write in your journal, and to apply the tips we've given you in this book, on how to make the most of your quiet time.

➢ During this devotional time, it is always good to think about: What does this teach me about

God, His Son, or His Holy Spirit? What does it teach me about myself? What applications can I apply so that this lesson from His Word can become more personal? This can be compared to "looking in the mirror" and seeing your reflection in God's Word... and even more... seeing the reflection of God as He reveals Himself (and HIS HEART) to you in a more personal manner, so that you can grow deeper in your relationship with Him, and then be a light to others.

The 2nd way to approach your study time is in a "Survey Study for Knowledge and Understanding." This is when you come before God and say, *"Lord, teach me so that I can understand the meat of Your Word."* You can do this as a Book Study, Chapter Study, Word Study, or a Topical Study.

This type of studying can be considered as a "Synthetic Bible Study" meaning to gain a general knowledge of its contents for overall historical understanding, and to gain a better appreciation of the original content and meaning. At this time, you are "looking at the BIG picture" and grasping the whole (or meat) of what was said, and why. This study time tends to lead to a broader view and more knowledge of the Word, whereas in your "devotional study time" you are zooming in to see up close and personal.

When you sit down for this "Survey for Knowledge-- Study Time," it should be looked at as a time set aside to "dig deeper" into His Word (and maybe even use this time to do a "formal Bible study" written by a Biblical teacher). Whereas your devotional study time is more heartfelt, and a time to feed your spirit; this time is for you to apply your ear as a *student of the Word*, so that God can teach YOU, so that you can grow not only WITH Him, but IN Him. This not only strengthens your own faith, but also will help you to be able to share what YOU have learned with others, thereby helping to strengthen their faith. Also, the reason this type of study time is so important, is so that YOU can come before God to, "search His Word", and know for certain the truth of His Word, thereby protecting yourself from falling under the influence of "false teaching."

This kind of study can be done as:
- A Full Book
- Chapter Studies
- Paragraph Studies

- Word Studies
- Biographical Studies
- Theological Study

> *From a detailed looked at these types of studies (and other ways to go deeper in God's Word), we invite you to consider reading our series on "Growing with God."*

As you prepare to sit down and *study* His Word, it is a good idea to have at least TWO different Bibles (in different versions) with you (even if it is one in front of you on your lap and one on the computer). The reason being is that it is a good idea to have them "side by side" so that you can compare the verses to get a better understanding of its full meaning. The different versions are going to state the words somewhat differently, and so by comparing them, it helps to build awareness. For instance, a while back, I was studying 1 Samuel 13 in my NASB, and I noticed that it started by saying, **"Saul was *thirty* years old when he began to reign, and he reigned forty two years over Israel. Now Saul chose for himself 3,000 men of Israel..."** (Vs. 1-2).

However, when I compare it to my NKJV Bible it says, **"Saul reigned one year; and when he had reigned two years over Israel, Saul chose for himself three thousand men of Israel."**

So why the difference? Because the original Hebrew text literally states this verse as, "Saul was years old when he began to reign, and he reigned two years over Israel." Since some of the Hebrew wording was difficult to decipher, when the translations into English began, this verse was compared to what the LXX had written (the early Greek translation of the Old Testament), and that of the Hebrew wording in 2 Sam. 5:4, 2 Kings 14:2, 2 Sam. 2:10, and also what Acts 13:21 stated. The 2011 text edition of the ESV Bible states the verse this way: **Saul lived for one year and then became king, and when he had reigned for two years over Israel, Saul chose three thousand men of Israel...."** The reference for the ESV acknowledges what the Hebrew text stated *"Saul was years old..."* and also what the LXX states, but it also goes on to list their corresponding verse with 1 Sam. 10:6. You see, after being anointed by Samuel, there were a series of events that Samuel predicted-- which came true-- one being that the Spirit of the Lord would come upon Saul and he would prophesy with some prophets, thus becoming a new man. Later, after this had happened, Saul was officially made king in public.

Now all Scripture is important, however the message we also need to remember is that of *the context* of what was being written and why... (This is why you need to read before -- and after-- the verses referenced in anything you are reading in study.) As you start to read 1 Samuel 13, it has been two years since Samuel had anointed Saul as king. Regardless of which translations you are reading, Saul's first year is acknowledged, but then it goes into what happened in his 2nd, because this is the year that defined what history would remember about him. You see, it was in his 2nd year that Saul went down to Gilgal as was previously predicted that he would. However, instead of WAITING for Samuel to join him, Saul took matters into his own hand and offered up the burnt offering, thus beginning his downfall.

On the onset of my study of 1 Samuel 13, and seeing the differences in these two Bibles (*which I knew to be word for word translations*), and then comparing them yet to another translation (the ESV), then doing a little research, it made me a more aware of the whole text. Plus,

I learned a little bit more about Biblical translation history that I had not known before. And all in all, by the time I was finished with 1 Samuel 13, I understood it more because it made me dig deeper as I looked at the whole chapter side by side through the different Bibles.

Something else to consider when you *study* your Bible is this: I always come to it with the thought of my camera. With a wide lens, I can see a lot-- I can also see distance. However, when I start zooming in, I begin to see more detail, and little things I missed when looking at a broader view. It is the same way with the Bible.

When you begin a study of any particular chapter, it is important to get a "broad view" to see the History behind it (basically the "big picture"). This gives an understanding of what happened at the time, and what the Scriptures are "capturing" in the telling of it. But then, as we start to "zoom in" we begin to see little things (and more detail). As we do this, we can begin to see a reflection of our lives and how it can be applied to us today. God's Word really is living-- it is NOT outdated!

Going back to 1 Samuel 13, let's look at a few things: First, none of Samuel's Words had proven wrong that Samuel had spoken to Saul before (see 1 Samuel 10). So when Saul found himself in Gilgal 2 years later (just as Samuel had said), he had no reason not to trust in what he had been told. He let men sway him into doing something God had not given him the authority to do. He obviously forgot about Gideon and his 300 men. If God could give Gideon victory WITH JUST A FEW, then He could do the same with Saul, and however few men were left. (So it didn't matter that so many were leaving in fear.)

Second, was that Samuel had told Saul to wait seven days. Saul waited, but on the 7th day when there was still no sign of Samuel, Saul took matters into his own hands, and as he finished guess who showed up! You see, Saul didn't wait the entire full 7 days, and even if Samuel had been delayed for an extra day, it still wasn't something God had designated Saul to do. He let his fear (and men) dictate to him instead of standing firm in what God had told him-- thus showing where his heart really lay. It also showed his true character.

So zooming in on this, how can it be applied to our lives? By considering the following: How often do we let other people influence us and dictate our stance? How often are we willing to let everyone else go off, but we stand FIRM on the instructions God has given us? How often do we "Go" when God told us to "WAIT?" We have to remember that God is all-powerful, and when He says WAIT, then it doesn't matter how dire the situation can get, because HE can do a MIGHTY thing even at the last moment, and with very little. *And lastly*, how often do we jump ahead and do things that we were NEVER appointed to do. How many times do we take it out of God's hand, or try to do something that someone else is appointed to do?

When studying God's Word, there is always a "then and there" and a "here and now." By this, I mean there is always an important lesson to be learned from the bigger picture, and from what the people who went before us did (be it success or failure). And there is a reflection, we can see in our lives, if we will but hold the light up and peer in a little bit closer.

───────────────────

One other thing about your study time: take the time to find all the related chapters in the Bible to the chapter (or verse) you are studying. By looking at the context of it from the different writers, you will see the whole picture, thus you will be able to grasp the lesson (meaning) behind it more. For example, when reading about the different kings of Judah and Israel in the Book of 1 Kings and 2 Kings; it is really important to find their counterparts in the 2 Chronicles to see how the whole story fits together. *(This is another reason it is nice to have two Bibles side by side-- so you don't have to keep flipping your pages back and forth.)* You will notice, for instances, in 1 Kings 15:3 we read that Azariah (King of Judah) did right in the eyes of the Lord. However, in verse 5, it says the Lord afflicted him with leprosy. This would seem odd, but it you study 2 Chronicles 26:16-22, you will learn what happened, and see that he became very prideful and it was his downfall.

Also, document insights" God shows you so that you won't forget them later. (There is a section for this at the end of this Book. Plus, you can print out a worksheet from our resource site and put them in a 3-ring binder—or just use notebook paper to write on-- and then use dividers to section them off. This way you can add to your notes as you grow in His Word.)

One other thing, when using a study Bible, or commentaries…. Be selective on what you read and take for truth. Always make sure that you let the BIBLE be your greatest commentary! Let Scripture back up what is being told to you (or rather, make sure that Scripture backs up the information you are reading.) For instances, if you are in a hurry during your reading, you might think that in Numbers 17:6 (where it is talking about the staffs for the tribes) that they're 13 staffs because Aaron's was included... there are some commentaries that even state 13 staffs... HOWEVER, if you study the whole passage (and even compare the passage in different translations), you will find that in verse 2 God told Moses to collect 12 staffs-- one to represent each tribe. The names of the tribal leaders were to be written on the staffs. You see, people were questioning Aaron's appointment, and God decided to show whom His chosen servant was. In verse 3, God told Moses to write Aaron's name on the staff of Levi's (meaning that Aaron was to represent the tribe of Levi). God said there should be 1 staff for the head of each house-- which makes for 12 staffs, *not 13*. The passage goes on to show the collecting of all the staffs, and that the staff with Aaron's name on it (which represented the tribe of Levi) bloomed; showing that he was God's chosen person.

When taking time to personally study the Bible, take into consideration the following for your study notes (don't forget to keep an eye out for your "hidden treasures" as well):

From the Old Testament

- Who are the main people in the passage, and what kind of relationship do they have with God?

- Are they being blessed or are they suffering? Are they being obedient? Is what they are going through because of previous disobedience?

- What are key verses in the passage, and what are other verse references related to it?

- What principal lesson can you apply to your own life?

From the Gospels

- Watch to see how Jesus relates Himself to God the Father (He KNOWS who He is).

- Pay attention to how He prays and speaks to the Father.

- Notice how Jesus is always aware of where His disciples are, and how He teaches them.

- Notice too, how often they miss-understand what He is saying to them.
- Watch how He shows His heart for people, and look at how others accept (and reject) Him.

If you would like more information on this series about strengthening your relationship with God and letting Him work to renew your heart and grow in His Word, we invite you to visit us at www.reflectionsofheart.com.

And also
www.growingingodsword.com

Below is a list on links we invite you to visit that for more information on our studies series, devotionals, newsletters, and Cypress Ministries.

Have a wonderful and blessed day!
Sincerely,
Your friends in Christ from
Cypress Ministries

hppt://www.cypressministries.com
http://www.lamppostpublications.com
http://www.thepathwayoffaithbookstore.com
http://www.reflectingonhisword.com
http://www.todaysdailydevotional.com

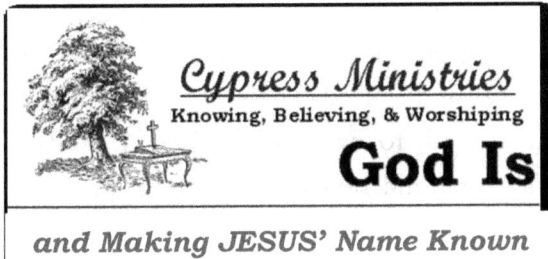

Cypress Ministries
Knowing, Believing, & Worshiping
God Is
and Making JESUS' Name Known

"For I proclaim the name of the Lord: ascribe greatness to our God. He is the Rock, His work is perfect; for all His ways are justice, a God of truth and without injustice; righteous and upright is He" (Deut 32:1-4 NKJV).

First and foremost we seek, with all our hearts, to honor and glorify God with our lives in all that we do. It isn't about making us known, but to make HIM known. We have a deep desire to help others who are seeking to grow in their daily walk with God, while learning to listen to the leading of God's Holy Spirit; and simply coming to know God, to believe what He says and to worship Him, because He Is God.

Cypress Ministries is the writing and leadership ministry of the Pathway of Faith foundation. Our main focus is on feeding those who are hungry, and thirsty for a deeper relationship with God the Father (and the Way of Christ), through the teaching of His Word. Though our primary call is to "feed God's people" we have a deep burden as well, to bring a message of HOPE to the brokenhearted and downcast, to show them that all is NOT lost, and that through Jesus Christ there IS spiritual health and healing, and eternal life.

**For more information on
Cypress Ministries
Please visit us at
www.cypressministries.com
www.pathwayoffaith.com**

♥♥♥♥♥♥♥♥♥♥♥♥

In following Jesus' example,
we are searching for God's lost people,
ministering to the disappointed, the hurt, and the lonely,
gently reminding them that Jesus is the way.

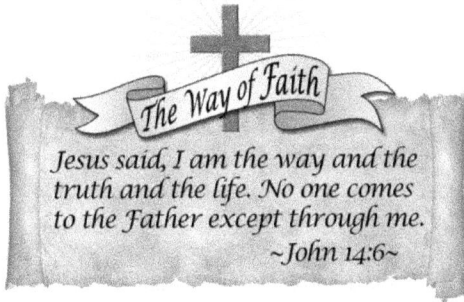

The Way of Faith

Jesus said, I am the way and the truth and the life. No one comes to the Father except through me.
~John 14:6~